The Life and Times of Alexander Keith

Nova Scotia's Brewmaster

Peter L. McCreath

FOUR
EAST
PUBLICATIONS

Published by
Four East Publications
P.O.B. 29
Tantallon, Nova Scotia B0J 3J0

2nd printing November 2001

edited by Richard Rogers
layout and design by Brenda Conroy and Richard Rogers
printed in Canada

Front cover visuals supplied by the Oland Brewery and reproduced courtesy of the Public Archives of Nova Scotia.
Highland cattle on acknowledgements page courtesy of the British Travel Association.
The First Ship for America, Acadian Recorder, Saturday July 26, 1817 and Alexander Keith advertisement, Acadian Recorder, Saturday, July 7, 1821 are reproduced courtesy of the Public Archives of Nova Scotia.
Back cover visual of bottles in cabinet reproduced courtesy of the Oland Brewery.

National Library of Canada Cataloguing in Publication Data
McCreath, Peter L.
The life & times of Alexander Keith, Nova Scotia's brewmaster

Includes bibliographical references.
ISBN 0-920427-56-1
1. Keith, Alexander, 1795-1873. 2. Brewers-Nova Scotia-Biography. 3. Politicians-Nova Scotia-Biography.
4. Freemasons-Nova Scotia-Biography. 5. Businessman-Nova Scotia-Biography. 6. Philanthropists-Nova Scotia-Biography.
I. Title.
FC2346.26.K44M33 2001 971.6'02'092 C2001-901564-X
F1039.5.H17K44 2001

To the immigrants who, like Alexander Keith, made our country what it is today; with special recognition to the Scots who, like my own ancestors, contributed so much to making Nova Scotia what it is today.

View of Halifax from Dartmouth Cove, 1829.

Collection of the Art Gallery of Nova Scotia.

Acknowledgements

The author wishes to express his thanks and appreciation to the staff of the Public Archives of Nova Scotia for their patience and assistance, to Irene Lane of the Oland Brewery for her support and assistance, to David Flemming for sharing his advice and knowledge, to Donald Keith, Arthur Keith, Jr., Greg Keith for sharing their knowledge of their families past, to the staff of the Art Gallery of Nova Scotia, especially Dianne O'Neill and Judy Dietz, and Richard Rogers of Four East Publications for his wisdom and confidence. The author has made every effort to credit the work of others for information, ideas and opinions sourced from their work. Errors or omissions are entirely the responsibility of the author.

Contents

Introduction

To Atlantic Canadians, the name "Alexander Keith" is synonymous with "beer," not just good beer, but the best, Alexander Keith's India Pale Ale. And, as they say, "those who like it, like it a lot!"

In fact, there was a lot more to Alexander Keith than brewing what has become Nova Scotia's most popular beer. Alexander Keith came to Nova Scotia as a young man from his native Scotland by way of northern England. He soon found a job as brewmaster with a local firm. Before long, he bought the brewery, expanded it and moved it to a new location—a location that today is the oldest brewing site still producing beer in Canada.

Alexander Keith became a leading member of the Halifax community, in the world of business, as well as in politics and community service. Twice he served as Mayor of Halifax. He served as President of the Province's Legislative Council. He was a leader in the Masonic Order, the North British Society and Highland Society of Nova Scotia. And, he was a devoted husband (twice) and father (nine times!).

In the words of one chronicler of 19th century Nova Scotia, Alexander Keith was "the most hospitable man who ever lived in this city (Halifax)"[1].

This is the story of Alexander Keith, his times and his legacy to Nova Scotians and the Maritimes.

CHAPTER ONE

Early Years

Alexander Keith was born October 5, 1795, in the village of Halkirk, County Caithness and Sunderland on the northern tip of Scotland. Halkirk borders on the Thurso River, six miles from the town of Thurso. Young Alexander was the second of four sons of Donald Keith and Christina Brims. Mr. Keith, Senior, died in Halkirk on September 21, 1847, in full knowledge of the success not only his son Alexander, but his son, John and his own brother David, had achieved in Nova Scotia.

The Clan Keith was and is both large and eminent in Scottish history. Surprisingly, it is not of Scottish origin. In fact, it's origins have been traced to the Thuringia region of Germany where the Keiths' warlike ancestors, a people called the Chattie, were forced out of what is now Germany by the Legions of Augustus Caesar under the command of his grandson-in-law Germanicus Cezr. The Chattie originally went to what is now Holland. But again, their warlike reputation made them unpopular with their neighbours. So, they took to the sea and headed for Britain. Blown north by a storm, they ended up on the shores of northern Scotland, settling in the area, which came to be known as Chatt-ness, or, more recently, Caithness.

The Chatti were considered dangerous invaders by the local Scottish population, who tried, unsuccessfully, to force them out. They were forced inland to the area from whence our Alexander Keith came several hundred years later. The Chatti remained a separate people, under their own ruler or prince, resident in northern Scotland for several hundred years. They were not allowed to marry or have any relations whatsoever with the Scots.

That attitude changed at the turn of the second millennium A.D., when the Chatti came to the support of the Scottish King Malcolm the 2nd, and helped him defeat an invading force of Danes at Camus in what is now the County of Angus. As a reward and thanks, Malcolm granted the Chatti leader several lands, including the Barony of Keith in East Lothian. Thereafter, the family took the name Keith, which has been the surname of his

Memorial to Robert the Bruce at Bannockburn.
Courtesy of the British Tourist Authority.

descendents ever since.

In 1176, a Keith was appointed Marischal (Marshal) of Scotland, the official custodian of the Royal regalia and protector of the King in Parliament. As of 1305, Sir Robert de Keith was a confident of the King of England, and represented Scotland at the Council in Westminster. He remained a supporter of the English King up until the invasion of Scotland by Edward I in 1314, which caused him to return his loyalties to his Scottish homeland.

He served as commander of Bruce's cavalry on that glorious

day at the Bannockburn. By a well-timed charge upon the English archers, he made a decisive contribution to the Scottish victory that day. Following the Battle of Bannockburn, Robert the Bruce rewarded Keith's loyalty with a large land grant in Aberdeenshire. Shortly thereafter, his fortunes were further enhanced by his marriage to the daughter of Bruce's brother-in-law. This alliance provided great estates in Kincardineshire, including the rock of Dunnottar, on which he built a great castle. This became the seat of his power, and he was appointed hereditary Marischal.

The title was then passed down through the family chain. In 1485, the incumbent Sir William Keith was created Earl Marischal and Lord Keith. The power of the Keith family continued to grow until 1715. In that year, the tenth and last Earl Marischal, the 22-year old George Keith, together with his brother James, supported the Jacobite cause against the House of Orange, then Hanover. The title and all lands were forfeited, costing George Keith all his assets and an annual income of 1676 pounds sterling a year.

Keith escaped to the continent, where he eventually surfaced first as a general in the Prussian army, then as Prussian Ambassador to Spain. In 1759, he secured a pardon from the King of England, and returned to Scotland, where he managed to re-purchase some of his former lands. He declined the King's invitation to resume his former titles. Instead, he returned to Prussia to live out his life in retirement. He died at the age of 86 in 1778.

One partcularly notable member of the Clan Keith was the Scottish poet and friend of King James VI of Scotland (Ist of England), Sir William Alexander. In 1621, he was granted a charter by James to establish a colony in North America to be named New Scotland, or as we know it, Nova Scotia!

Several Keiths died in the

Sir William Alexander.
Courtesy of the New Brunswick Museum.

Scottish cause at the Battle of Culloden in 1745. Today, the 13th Earl of Keith resides at Keith Hall estate in Aberdeenshire.

Halkirk was originally settled by Norse emigrants about a thousand years ago. Indeed, the word "Halkirk" is derived from the Norse word for "high church." By the time that Alexander Keith was a young boy, in 1803, Halkirk had become one of the first planned villages in the Scottish Highlands. Even today, the grid pattern of the streets reflects that original plan.

Today, Halkirk still boasts a couple of castles, hosts one of the biggest annual Highland Games in Scotland, and claims to be one of the best places to fish salmon and trout in Britain. Legend has it that a fortune in gold is buried at the bottom of the pond next to the cemetery just beyond the quarry, all that remains of Dirlot Castle, the 14th century home of Sir Reginald De Cheyne.

The father of Alexander Keith was a respected farmer and chief of the clan Keith.[2] The elder Keith, as was not uncommon in Scotland, then as now, believed strongly in education. Accordingly, young Alexander received an excellent education before going down the road to pursue his future and seek his fortune.

Highland Regiments.

Public Archives of Canada.

A ruined medieval castle in Scotland.

Courtesy of the British Tourist Authority.

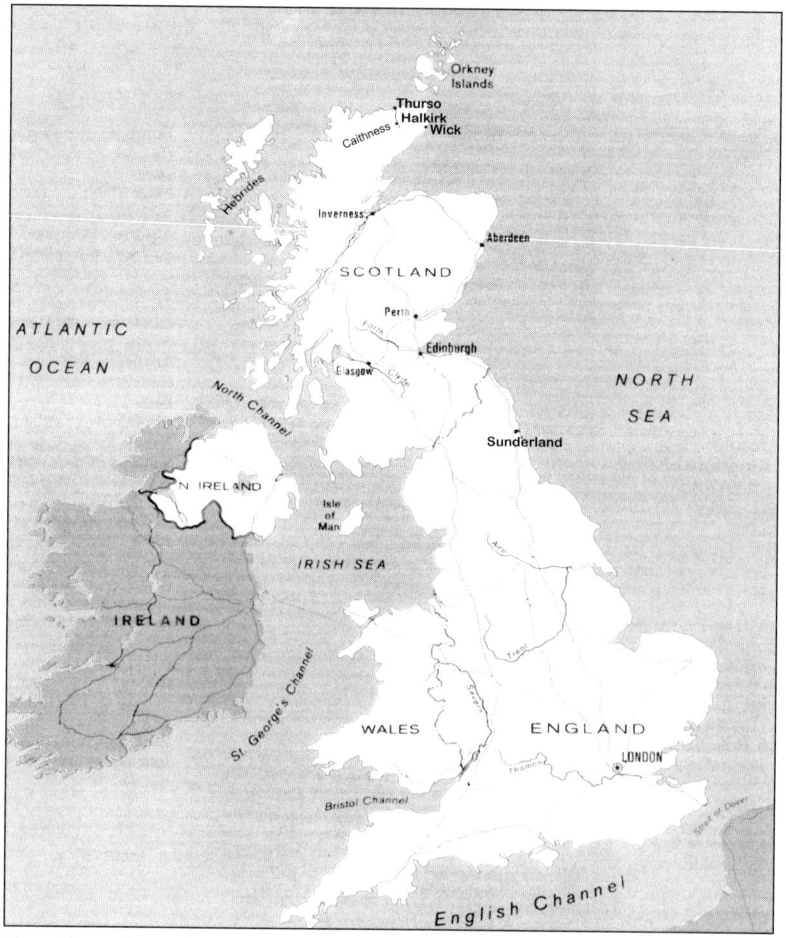

Scotland and England

CHAPTER 2

Becoming a Brewmaster

In 1812, 17-year old Alexander was sent, by his father, to Sunderland, in northern England, to be apprenticed to his uncle in the brewing trade, and to learn about the beer and malt business. At the time, Sunderland was one of the major brewing areas of England, with four large and eight small breweries. Although little is known about this period of Keith's life, he apparently spent periods of time, as well, gaining valuable experience in both London and Edinburgh.

Beer was an important part of the diet and culture of the British Isles, then as now. It was during this period, in fact, that the particular type of beer for which Alexander Keith is so famous, India Pale Ale, was developed.

Beer is one of the oldest manufactured forms of nourishment known to civilization. It has been well documented that the ancient Egyptians made "strong and excellent" beer as early as 2,000 B.C.[1] Beer-making in ancient times was not complicated: "To make beer you moisten barley (or some other grain), keep it moist until it germinates, then heat the grain to stop the germination (the result is called malt), and finally add water and yeast so the malt sugars ferment." The product is beer![2] The ancient Egyptians even gave names to their favourite beers, names such as "Joy Bringer" or "the Beautiful and Heavenly"[3]

The name 'India Pale Ale' really did originate in India.

During the 18th century, England was known for its great navy. Ships of the Royal Navy sailed the world, and made possible the great British Empire. But in so doing, the Royal Navy faced a serious problem: beer didn't keep well on long voyages, especially on long voyages to hot or tropical climates. In such places, beer would go flat and take on a sour, unpleasant taste. Aside from the fact that beer drinking was an important part of British culture, and was a substance close to every sailor's heart, beer was considered important to maintaining the health of sailors during long periods at sea. For example, it was a ready source

A view of Halifax from Fort George, Nova Scotia, 1817.
Collection of Art Gallery of Nova Scotia.

of vitamin B. Beer was considered so important that every day at sea, each man was issued a ration of one gallon of beer for his own consumption. This was easy in the northern waters of Europe, such as the English Channel or the North Sea, where beer could be kept cold, and where ships frequently and easily could return to English ports for replenishment.

By the 18th century, the ships of the Royal Navy sailed the world, and the British saw India as a limitless source of wealth for years to come. Not only did ships frequently visit India, an entire fleet was stationed there. So, the great problem became where to get beer.[4] Various experiments were conducted in trying to create concentrates to which local water could be added to make beer during long periods away from home. But, this only worked in colder climates. The problem of supplying beer in the tropics remained. In fact, it was this problem that led the Royal Navy, about 1740, to begin to use rum as a substitute for beer. Because of its higher alcohol content, it was already a concentrate, and could be mixed quite pleasantly with water or fruit juices. Beer was still considered healthier, but from then on the Navy had switched to rum.

Not so the army, nor the colonists, who started to settle in places like India. Unfortunately, hot climates were no more conducive to making beer than to storing it. Some solution to the great beer problem had to be found if Englishmen were to continue to enjoy their beer, even in places like India.

It was a man called George Hodgson, a brewer from the Bow Brewery in East London, who came up with the solution. During the 1790s, he developed a new recipe for making beer.

He called the product Hodgson's India Ale, a variation of the ale he had been making in London for 40 years. Hodgson's 'ales' were lighter in colour than the brown ales, porters and stouts that were popular at that time. Hodgson's discovery lay in his use of alcohol and hops,[5] which were the key to preventing spoilage. The higher the levels of alcohol and hops that the beer contained, the less friendly an environment it provided for the development of bacteria and other components that could spoil the beer. Tomlinson indicates that "Hodgson took his pale ale recipe, increased the hop content considerably, and raised the starting specific gravity through the addition of extra grain and sugar".[6] In a nutshell, the higher the alcohol content, the longer it lasted.

Naturally, Hodgson's India Ale quickly captured the colonial market. Before long, others figured out Hodgson's secret and began brewing their own India Pale Ale. By the time Alexander Keith took up the brewing trade, India Pale Ale dominated the lucrative export market.

After five years learning his craft and trade in Northern England, along with gaining valuable experience in London and Edinburgh, Alexander Keith decided to leave Britain. He sailed to Halifax, Nova Scotia, to seek fame and fortune in the new world. Little did he know just how successful he would be, for it was in Nova Scotia that he would find both fame and fortune.

Keith was by no means alone in deciding that there would be greater opportunity in the Colonies of British North America, than at home in the United Kingdom. This was particularly true of Highland Scots for whom economic opportunity had been greatly diminished by what is called the enclosure movement of the late 18th and early 19th centuries. Industrialization created a great demand for raw wool for the great woolen mills of England and the Lowlands of Scotland. Mutton was also in growing demand as a popular dish. Landlords in the Scottish Highlands soon realized that there was more money to be made in raising sheep than in leasing land to subsistence farmers for small rents. So many cleared their land of tenant farmers, who were thus forced to find opportunities and homes elsewhere. Some went to cities in the south, like Glasgow. Others looked across the Atlantic to America. For many, it became a choice between leaving home, or facing starvation by staying.

The decision to consider America was not entirely based on being forced from their homes. Many realized that if they could eek out a living from the barren and inhospitable soil on a small patch of the Scottish Highlands, perhaps a grand living could be had in the fertile lands of British North America—especially, when offers of free land and talk of further incentives abounded. And indeed, many, like Alexander Keith, succeeded in the Colonies, including Nova Scotia.[7]

Many who sailed to Nova Scotia were enticed either by letters from friends and relatives, or by advertising flyers circulated widely in home areas of hardship.

"THE FIRST SHIP FOR AMERICA.

For Halifax & Prince Ed. Island, the beautiful fast-sailing ship New-Brunswick Packet, burthen 600 tons, copper-fastened and coppered to the bends, James Walker, master, will sail hence for the above Ports the first of May, and as most of the Passengers are already engaged, an early application will be necessary. For Freight or Passage apply to Mr. John M'Cleery, Broker, or to James Wilson,
Derry, March 31, 1817. Thomas Lindsay

There is no part of the Continent of America that affords so great encouragement to Mechanicks, Farmers, and Labourers as what British America does; on arrival out, an application being made to the Governor, grants of Land from 200 to 1000 Acres will be made out for EVER, according to the number in each respective Family.—Mechanicks can earn 8 to 12 Dollars per Week, and Labourers six to seven shillings per day."

Now Mr. Editor, if any of your readers will take the trouble to go to Belcher's wharf, they will *see this "beautiful and fast-sailing ship"* described as *"copper fastened and coppered to the bends and of 600 Tons burthen,"* an old worm-eaten ves-

Published accounts by successful settlers, who took it upon themselves to share their success and what they saw as great opportunities for others, influenced many, as did promotional materials published by colonial governments seeking new, enterprising, ambitious and hardworking immigrants. Any of these inducements might have encouraged Keith to make his decision to go to Halifax. Often emigrants decided in advance exactly where they were going, based on the materials they had seen, or specific inducements they had been offered.

Following the Napoleonic Wars, there was a major wave of emigration to Nova Scotia. It was a wave that continued for twenty years, reaching a peak between 1826 and 1831. As the war came to a close, local authorities and community leaders in Nova Scotia particularly welcomed immigrants from "the old country." At the same time, the Imperial Government saw emigration to the colonies as one solution to the explosive growth of population amongst the urban poor of Britain, as well as providing a greater market in the colonies for British manufactured goods.

In his book on immigration to Nova Scotia, 1815-1838,[9] J. S. Martell documents that approximately 43,000 immigrants came to Nova Scotia during the post War of 1812 period. He breaks down their origins as follows:

United Kingdom	37,500
Newfoundland	1,700
United States, Quebec & New Brunswick	1,400
Black refugees from the United States	1,700*
Demobilized soldiers from British Forces	700

*It is interesting to note that Martell distinguishes the black immigrants from the United States from other immigrants from that country. These people were, invariably, escaped slaves from the Southern United States. Following the war, the American government demanded their return, as they considered slaves to be property. The British government refused—after all, aside from the fact that Britain was moving toward the banning of slavery throughout the British Empire (it would come in 1833, and indirectly prove to bring significant economic benefit to Alexander Keith and his counterparts in the brewing industry, by undermining the plantation system of the Caribbean through which the sugar that was the basis of cheap rum was produced!). As during the American Revolution, the British had offered freedom to any slaves who either joined the British Forces, or came to the loyal colonies. However, after 1814, the Americans did not give up on the matter, and eventually it was arbitrated by the Czar of Russia in 1818. He prevailed upon the British to pay $1,000,000 in compensation to the Americans for the approximately 3000 slaves who had settled in British North America.[10]

These figures only reflect people arriving at Halifax, Sydney and Pictou. Martell estimated that another 10,000 to 20,000 immigrants landed elsewhere, where no note was taken of their arrival. Off-setting these numbers are those who died soon after arrival, or who emigrated to the United States or elsewhere.

The population of Nova Scotia was about 75,000 in 1815 and 200,000 in 1838. Martell estimated that about 85,000 of the increase of 125,000 occurred through natural growth, leaving about 40,000 or so to result from immigration.

Having decided to emigrate to Nova Scotia, or other Colonies, the prospective immigrants then had to face the North Atlantic. This could be a long and, at times, perilous journey. Not all vessels made it across the Atlantic, though as the years went by, the voyages took less time and the ships were safer. However, few could be described as comfortable. Passengers often had to live in cargo areas of ships designed for transporting timber and logs. In effect, they were used as ballast for the return voyage from the UK. Conditions were often uncomfortable and unsanitary, and the food poor. In some cases, passengers were actually required to bring their own food for the trip across the ocean.

Paying a handsome sum to make the voyage provided no guarantee that the port of disembarkation would be that indicated at the beginning of the voyage. The port of arrival and disembarkation might be changed en route to reflect the convenience and cargo opportunities determined by the ship's captain.

Alexander Keith was not alone as an ambitious, but not very wealthy immigrant from Scotland in 1817. Over half of the immigrants who came to Nova Scotia during the period were Scots, and over half of the immigrants who came to Nova Scotia entered the province through the port of Halifax. Most of these

Passengers on board an emigration vessel.
Public Archives of Canada/C-6556

Scots came from the Highlands (as did Keith) or the Western Isles.

In Keith's case, it is quite possible that he did not come on one of the six ships that arrived at Halifax from Scottish ports during 1817, bringing with them some 600 prospective Nova Scotians. On July 5, 1817, a ship called the "Kirkaldy" arrived from northern England and disembarked 93 passengers. If Alexander Keith came directly from Sunderland, it is possible that he came on this voyage.

Keith's journey could not have been substantially different than that of other immigrants from the UK at that time. Fortunately, conditions on board ships were not as horrendous as they would be for desperate emigrants from the Irish famine 25 years later. Still, it meant a long voyage on an uncertain, and at times terrifying sea in small sailing ships, which were often less than a thousand tons.

Becoming an immigrant meant leaving home. It meant having to be prepared to adjust to a new environment, a new culture and a new way of life.

Wreck of the emigrant ship *JOHN.*

Collection of the Art Gallery of Nova Scotia.

Halifax Weather at the Time of Keith's Arrival

How did Halifax weather in the early 19th century compare with that of today? Here's one man's description: The summers were hotter and the winters colder … Our springs, the worst period of the year, did not then linger as they now [1912] do into June but sprang into maturity in May. I have frequently known the first day of May, then almost invariably commemorated by the community as a day for gathering the sweet little natal flowers, to be uncomfortably hot, while now the pretty Mayflower has a struggle to raise its pretty head above the remaining rifts of snow. From May until October, the weather was warm and during the months of June, July, August and September almost tropical in its temperature. November was as dreary and chilly as it has since as a rule continued to be, and in December we had our first fall of snow which from that time, with the exception of the January thaw covered the ground with a heavy coating varying from three to six feet [1 to 2 metres], until about the end of March. But the winter notwithstanding its severity was a merry time [!] [11]

Today, Canada is a nation of immigrants, and the sons and daughters of immigrants. For each person who chooses or is forced to leave home to test the future in a new land, there is excitement, fear, challenge, uncertainty, opportunity and peril. Alexander Keith came with little in the way of financial resources. But, he was fortunate to bring a solid education, a skilled trade, the drive, energy and determination of a true entrepreneur, and the good fortune to speak the local language on arrival, and he shared the heritage of a substantial portion of the population of 'New Scotland.'

The English and Newfoundland Mail Vessels Making their Way through the Ice in Halifax Harbour, 1859.

Collection of the Art Gallery of Nova Scotia.

Tandem Club assembling in front of Dalhousie College, Halifax, Nova Scotia, 1842.

Collection of Art Gallery of Nova Scotia.

CHAPTER 3

Becoming a Halifax Business Leader

Shortly after his arrival at Halifax, Keith found employment, and a wonderful opportunity, as the sole brewer and business manager for Charles Boggs, a local merchant and trader. Boggs, himself, was not a brewmaster, although his was the oldest brewery in Halifax. Beer and ales had been brewed in Halifax for many years. Nevertheless, Alexander Keith was probably the first highly qualified brewmaster to take up residence and ply his craft in Halifax.[1] Within three years, Keith was in a position to buy the brewery from Boggs, and became his own man, and the brewery's sole proprietor.

The Halifax to which Keith came in 1817 was a community in transition. Established in 1749 as a military counterpoise to the great French fortress of Louisbourg, Halifax remained a military town and the site of the naval dockyard. Since the establishment of Halifax, Britain had been at war more than at peace. Because of its strategic importance, Halifax was a port that thrived on war. With the end of the Napoleonic Wars in 1815, with the demise of French power, and with the end of hostilities with the United States (known in Canada as the War of 1812, in which Nova Scotians had been actively involved), many people in Halifax wondered what the future had in store. Up to that time, Halifax's prosperity had been linked to war. Could it survive and grow in peace?[2]

One example of the economic uncertainty of the time was the challenge of finding funding to give life to the newly established Dalhousie College. It had been established in 1818, and endowed with funds taken during the War in a raid on the customs house in Castine, Maine. However, by 1821, with the departure from Nova Scotia of the Governor, the Earl of Dalhousie, construction had come to a halt because of a lack of funds.[3]

By 1819, there were signs of recovery—even before a full-

Province House, Halifax, Nova Scotia.
Courtesy of the Public Archives of Nova Scotia.

scale recession could be underway. In that same year, Province House, the new home of the Nova Scotia Legislature and Supreme Court was completed. It is still in use today, and remains the oldest legislative chamber in continuous use in Canada.

Another example was the construction of the Shubenacadie Canal, which was intended to provide a transportation link between Halifax and the Bay of Fundy. Unfortunately, it was obsolete by the time it was complete. (It is interesting to note that Alexander Keith saw potential in its use for his business, and took out water lot leases and assembled land for a warehouse along the Bedford Shore.)

As well, new businesses appeared on the scene. Among them, one was advertised in the *Acadian Recorder* on July 7, 1821 as follows:

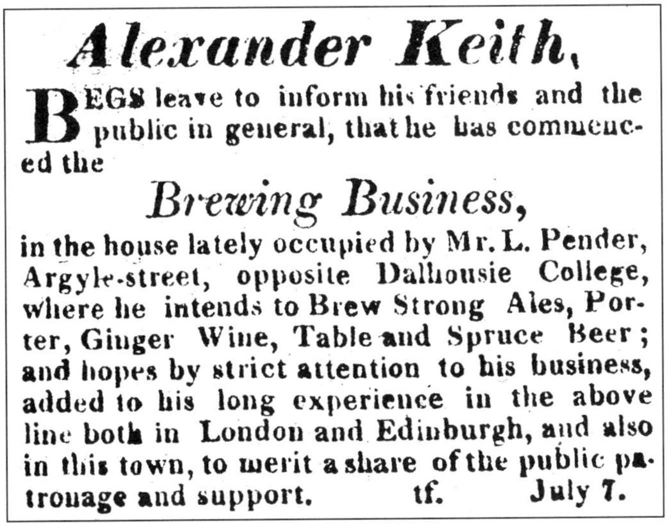
Alexander Keith,

BEGS leave to inform his friends and the public in general, that he has commenced the

Brewing Business,

in the house lately occupied by Mr. L. Pender, Argyle-street, opposite Dalhousie College, where he intends to Brew Strong Ales, Porter, Ginger Wine, Table and Spruce Beer; and hopes by strict attention to his business, added to his long experience in the above line both in London and Edinburgh, and also in this town, to merit a share of the public patronage and support. tf. July 7.

Keith's brewery came to be known as the "Nova Scotia Brewery." In its newspaper ads, it was officially dated from 1820, the year during which its ownership passed to Alexander Keith.

Keith's business grew quickly and steadily. Within two years, he concluded that he had outgrown his Argyle Street premises. In 1822, he announced the re-location of his brewery to a site on Lower Water Street (its present-day location). Keith purchased the property from Wm. Story and Sons, well-established local merchants, who, among other activities, had operated a brewery near the site in partnership with a firm called Lydiard and Story.[4] A large wooden structure was built to house the enterprise, and over the years extensions and outbuildings were added.

Between the military establishment, the navy, the naval dockyard, and the coming and going of merchant ships, there was no shortage of customers for Alexander Keith's very popular products. Added to these ever-thirsty individuals were the construction workers and others engaged in such major public works projects as the Halifax Citadel. This project took over twenty years to complete, commencing in 1828. In addition, there were other harbour defense fortification projects.[5]

The Soldiers' Smoking Room, 1872.

Collection of Art Gallery of Nova Scotia.

Due in no small measure to the military and naval establishment, the Halifax "aristocracy" (in other words, men of wealth and position—women were only accorded the status of their husbands or fathers) led a high and active social life, one to rival that of upper-crust London, no doubt. One of such background, reminiscing on the days of his youth many years later, described Halifax society, as he remembered it:

Halifax was a very gay town, and remarkable for the hospitality of its people and the beauty of its girls, the latter a reputation it has never lost. … The garrison consisted of three full regiments of foot, three batteries of artillery, and a large corps of Engineers … In the army a large proportion of the officers were men of wealth, … with the purchase system* there was a great inducement for rich men to enter the service … almost all from the parent country, and with proportionate incomes all living in much style, spending large amounts in the town, and giving a tone of great gaiety and profusion to the community.

But besides those sources of gaiety and amusement, there were ... numerous bodies of various descriptions, all of which were centers of conviviality. There were the officers of the several battalions of Militia, the different national societies, the fire companies, ... and the Free Masons. All of them had their annual ball for their wives, daughters and friends and their dinners for themselves.[6]

(*Note: "the purchase system" referred to the practice common in the British forces at that time whereby commissions in the army and navy could be purchased, rather than just earned on merit.)

Such was the life of the wealthy. Those less fortunate, of whom there were infinitely more, scraped to keep hearth and home together—especially during difficult years and cold winters. Not surprisingly, less is written of the lives of the unfortunate. The evidence of the challenges of survival faced by the poor, and the lack of support forthcoming from the community and government is often anecdotal. One example is the story of the three fishermen recalled in the reminiscences of an elderly chronicler just after the turn of the century.[7]

It seems that three fishermen from Herring Cove near Halifax had experienced a very poor harvest, such that they could not support their families. Nor could they find any alternate work. So, they decided to row to Halifax with the intention of begging for assistance from the various merchants of the city. Failing to receive either assistance or sympathy, they headed back to their boat to row home.

On the way, as they passed the yard of one of the merchants who had declined their appeal, one of the men saw three fancy waistcoats hanging from a line and stole them. Shortly thereafter, repenting his sin, he went with his two friends to return the goods. However, the merchant summoned the local constable, who, notwithstanding the remorse shown by the men, and the second thoughts of the merchant about seeing them charged, did his duty as he saw it. The men were duly charged before a magistrate and taken to jail. There they had to await the next session of the Supreme Court. No notice was sent to their families and it was not until some days later that one of the wives came looking for them in the city. She learned of their fate and visited her husband through the bars of the prison. In due course, the trial was held, the men pled guilty, and were condemned to death. In accordance with the justice of the day, the three were "hung by the neck until dead," and may God have had mercy on their souls. And, in the words of the chronicler: "A wise man was David when he said to God, 'Let me fall into the hands of the Lord and not into the hands of man'."

It should be noted, that sentences of death by hanging were carried out in public during early 19th century Halifax.

On March 15, 1834, a fire was set in a warehouse on Barrington Street owned by Alexander Keith. It resulted in considerable damage. A boarding house, operated on the upper floor of the building by a Mr. Paul, also sustained damage. On April 25, two women, Esther Ann Sutherland and Eleanor Smith were charged and brought before judge and jury, with the Attorney General, himself acting as prosecutor. In addressing the jury, the prosecutor said: "the offence for which the prisoners were indicted, was, he was happy to say, of rare occurrence in the coun-

The Fire in Granville Street, 1859.
Collection of Art Gallery of Nova Scotia.

try." The crime of arson was a capital offence at that time in the British Empire. He also noted that in Saxon times, punishment for this crime, which was considered much more serious than theft, was burning. After all, it led to loss of life, thus amounted, in his judgment to murder.[8]

The trial was an extensive one, and sordid to say the least. Mrs. Sutherland claimed to have been abandoned by her husband. He, in turn, was indebted to Alexander Keith as well as to the owners of the other two properties burned. The disappearance of the husband meant that his property was forfeit to the creditors. It appeared that the arson was an act of retribution committed by the disgruntled and vengeful Mrs. Sutherland. However, having heard the evidence presented, the Chief Justice concluded that there was insufficient evidence to convict the accused on so serious a charge. As a result, he instructed the jury to acquit the accused—which they did. It is interesting to note that in dismissing the accused, the Chief Justice clearly implied that he believed the two women to be guilty, and counseled them not do it again! For their part, Keith and the other victims received little satisfaction from the judicial proceedings.

There is no evidence that crime was more common in Halifax than in other places of the time. Since the establishment of Halifax in 1749, justice had been dispensed by two levels of officers: Justices of the Peace (JPs), who were neither paid nor trained in the law, and Justices of the Supreme Court, who were well-paid and had been trained, thus were learned in the law. The latter handled all criminal cases and all civil cases involving more than three pounds sterling.[9]

The increased wealth that came to Halifax during and after the Napoleonic Wars led to fears amongst the wealthy that the community required more legal enforcement. Taxes were raised to support the office of Police Magistrate and to pay for the hiring of three new police constables under his command. As well, a Halifax Police Court was established to deal with criminal cases for crimes involving less than ten pounds. Gradually, the Police Magistrate's office evolved into a court and was referred to as the Halifax Police Court, which came to handle most criminal matters. The fact that the arson case of 1834 was heard by the Supreme Court reflected both the gravity of the

Money in Nova Scotia during the time of Alexander Keith

It is sometimes difficult to keep track of currencies as you travel from one country to another. It is just as difficult to figure out currencies from other eras.

Before switching to the decimal system, British currency was divided into Pounds (£), Shillings (s) and Pence (d). One pound comprised twenty shillings. Each shilling comprised 12 pence. There was also what was called a 'guinea', which consisted of a pound and a shilling.

In 1812, Nova Scotians began to establish their own currency, when the Legislature passed an Act "authorizing the appointment of three fit and proper persons as commissioners, to issue Treasury notes to the total amount of £12,000 each."The total amount would be issued in notes of denominations ranging from £1 to £50. These were interest-bearing bonds paying 6% per year beginning on the date of issue. And, of course, they were based on British currency. The new bonds were used as currency, especially for paying members of the military.

Within a year, these notes were called in by the government, which passed a new law establishing non-interest-bearing bonds, which could also be re-issued from one holder to the next. These new bonds were issued directly by the government which was supposed to have one Pound in gold for each Pound in bonds it issued. If, on demand, the government did not have the gold, it would be obligated to issue an interest-bearing bond in its place. Once banks were established in Halifax (the first being the Halifax Banking Company established in 1825 to encourage the less wealthy to save), they also issued notes that served as currency.

Many people lacked confidence in these paper notes. During the 1830s, currency became a major topic of debate in the Nova Scotia Legislature. Some proposed that Nova Scotia should formally adopt British currency as the currency of the Colony. Others thought that colonies should establish their own currency, with their own coins and notes. By 1846, Nova Scotia had passed 22 pieces of legislation relating to currency. In that year, a new pound note was issued to replace all others.

Coins had long been in circulation in Nova Scotia. In 1834, an Act was passed which established a single standard for valuing the various coins in circulation, such as the Spanish doubloon, the English shilling and the pound sterling as represented by a gold coin in the UK called a sovereign. The sovereign or one pound sterling was equal to 25 Shillings.

In 1862, the dollar was introduced to Nova Scotia with what was called "Halifax Currency." The dollar was to be the new standard of currency. Standard values were established for the conversion. For example:

Sovereign =	1 Pound Sterling =	$5
Doubloon =	3-4 Pounds Sterling =	$16
Silver Dollar =	4 Shillings 2 Pence =	$1.04
British Crown =	5 Shillings =	$1.25
Half Crown =	2 Shillings 6 Pence =	$.625
Florin =	2 Shillings =	$.50
Shilling =	1 Shilling =	$.25

Following Confederation, Nova Scotia adopted the currency of the new Dominion of Canada. Canadian Currency was essentially the same as that of Nova Scotia—only with new coins and notes issued by the new Government of Canada. So it remains today.[10]

charges and the value of the property involved. The Halifax Police Court remained in place, until it was replaced by a court comprised of the elected Mayor or Aldermen, after the incorporation of the city in 1841. Following Confederation, a system of paid judges was instituted.

On June 17, 1836, the cornerstone was laid for what would become the new Keith's Brewery, a large, solid granite structure, which remains to this day. The event was marked by a celebration, which included 60 of Keith's employees and friends. "Old British hospitality" was much in evidence.[11] The occasion was also marked by a newspaper comment that:

> The Establishment, when complete, will be first of the kind

Keith's Brewery, 1850.

Courtesy of the Public Archives of Nova Scotia

> in British North America; and it is to be hoped Mr. Keith's spirited example will be a stimulus to some of our wealthy citizens to arouse their dormant energies; that they may do good while they have opportunity, laying up in store a good foundation towards the attainment of eternal life.[12]

Once the expansion was complete, including the installation of the latest in equipment and technology, the Nova Scotia Brewery was as modern and productive as any in Halifax, producing a variety of products. Operating at capacity at mid-century, the plant produced 180 hogsheads of porter and ales during the eight 'cold' months and 240 hogsheads during the four summer months. (Note: a hogshead is 52.5 imperial gallons, or approximately 239 litres.) Annual consumption of barley was 15,000 bushels from Canada and Prince Edward Island, and 3,000 bushels of malt from Canada and Scotland. As well, 300 bales of hops were annually imported from Canada, the United States and England. Several dozen employees were continuously employed.

At the time, this expansion was considered somewhat of a risk. Only a few months earlier, Joseph Howe had written in the *Novascotian* that Halifax was facing challenging economic times. He noted the closing of several businesses, and that people would not sell their homes or businesses, except for cash. For Keith, it was a far-sighted decision, short-term pain for long term gain, as would be said today. With the expansion, most of the original Lower Water Street wooden building was replaced with a "massive ironstone and granite-fronted brick structure."[13] The stone was quarried at the "King's Quarries" along the shores of Purcell's Cove, the same stone that was used to build the Citadel and other military buildings. Further renovations were made to the structure in 1871.

In 1853, Keith's son, Donald G. Keith, became a partner, and the company's name was changed to "Alexander Keith & Son."[14] Naturally, Alexander looked forward to his son succeeding him in the business. But, as sometimes happens, the son could not match his father as an entrepreneur. Perhaps Donald was somewhat intimidated by the success and prominence of his father. In any event, he did not prove to have the interest, nor did he achieve the success that his father had. Following the death of Alexander

Margaret Louise (Keith) Wickwire's wedding picture, 1870.

Courtesy of Jocelyn Morash.

Keith, the success of the business steadily declined. Donald died in 1886 at the age of 43. Unmarried and childless, he was succeeded by his sister, Margaret Louise, who took control of the brewery. Margaret Louise's husband, Dr. William N.Wickwire eventually left his medical practice in Kings County to oversee the business.[15]

Dr. William N. Wickwire

Courtesy of the Public Archives of Nova Scotia

By the 1840s, Alexander Keith had become a very successful and respected business leader in Halifax. As a result, his advice, business acumen and leadership were sought by other enterprises. In 1837, he was invited and joined the Boards of Directors of the Bank of Nova Scotia and the Halifax Fire Insurance Company. The following year, he helped establish and joined the Board of the Halifax Marine Insurance Company. In 1844, he joined the Boards of the Colonial Life Assurance Company and the Halifax Gas, Light and Water Company, and in 1856, that of the Halifax Water Company.

One night in November, 1854, the Keith residence was one of three targeted by burglars. Keith was said to have lost 150 pounds sterling in cash. There is no indication that the perpetrators were ever apprehended.[16]

On September 2, 1863, Alexander Keith presided over the laying of the corner stone of his new residence. Buried within it was a sealed lead box which contained copies of local newspapers, plans for the building and a few coins of the day. Keith's wife, Eliza, using a special silver trowel, applied the first mortar. On careful scrutiny, and with the assistance of a square and level, Keith declared that the stone was properly laid. The Reverend Boyd blessed the building, thence three cheers were raised to the Queen. A thoughtful member of the audience also called for three cheers for Alexander Keith, which were roundly joined.

Residence of Hon. Alexander Keith, 1872.

Collection of the Art Gallery of Nova Scotia.

Then, all present adjourned for a lunch "in good old English style with roast beef, plum pudding and XXX ale."[17]

Some months later, when the house was completed, Keith hosted a major dinner for all the workmen who had worked on the construction. At that time, the house must have afforded as elegant and comfortable living as any in Halifax.

Keith Hall was designed by the Scottish architect, David Stirling. His work was very popular and admired in Halifax at that time.[18] Among other Halifax buildings designed by Stirling were the Halifax Club and the Art Gallery of Nova Scotia Building on Hollis Street. Keith Hall followed a pattern of design very popular for the homes of the affluent in 19th century Halifax. Similar buildings, at least in façade, can be seen even today, not only along Hollis Street, but also along the northern part of Brunswick Street, between Cogswell and North Streets. As described by Edith Creighton:

> (The façade) is symmetrical, its front door approached through an imposing enough area between two rather Corinthian pillars. There are decorative carvings above the doorway and windows, two windows on either side

Alexander Keith.

Courtesy of Don MacLean.

> of the entrance.
>
> The central hall still gets its light through the delicately bright painted glass of nearly a century ago...
> On each side of the spacious hall are doors whose frames are ornamented with graceful carved figures, once, doubtless, of rich dark wood, but now painted pure white. Part way up the curving stairway, one sees the large original window, depicting the Masonic sun of the grand master, and the coat of arms of the Hon. Alexander Keith.
> The ornate plastering of the cornices of the splendid rooms and the decorative centerpieces from which the lighting fixtures hang, still attest the skill of the plasterer's art in the Victorian age.
> The house was originally heated by an enormous hall stove, and by fireplaces in the rooms where beautiful white marble mantels allow one to see in imagination, cozy family gatherings, or groups of guests around a glowing fire.[19]

Keith Hall contains its own element of mystery. Attached to the house, and immediately to the north of it, is another built by Keith in 1835 (where the Keith family lived during the construction of Keith Hall). From this structure runs a tunnel leading directly to the brewery, which, itself, fronts on Lower Water Street. This tunnel is two stories below the level of Hollis Street.

For a period of time, early in the 20th century, Keith Hall fell into decline. However, it was used by the armed forces during World War II, and in 1947, was purchased by A. Keith and Son Ltd., and became the business headquarters of the Oland Brewery company. Today, it is the home of an established Halifax law firm.

The curving stairway inside Keith Hall.

Courtesy of the Oland Brewery.

Stained glass window on stairway inside Keith Hall.

Courtesy of the Oland Brewery.

Fireplace inside Keith Hall.

Courtesy of the Oland Brewery.

Shipping at Low Tide,
Halifax, c.1820.

Collection of the Art Gallery of Nova Scotia

CHAPTER 4

Politician and Public Leader

It is not an uncommon thing for business leaders to be recruited to provide leadership to their communities through public service. It's a natural fit. A leader is a leader, and those who excel in the business world naturally take a strong interest in the success and progress of the political and economic environment in which they do business. There is also often a sense of obligation to return, through voluntarism and public service, a little of what one has derived in personal wealth, success and satisfaction, from the economic opportunity and strength of the community. Such a man was Alexander Keith.

The 1830s and 1840s were a momentous time for reform of government in Nova Scotia. The period began with the "Brandy Election" of 1830, and a decision by the Legislative Assembly to re-impose an additional 4 pence per gallon tax on brandy. It was considered an additional tax because, while the Assembly had earlier voted to impose a tax of 2 shillings, 4 pence on brandy, the 4 pence had never actually been collected. The governing Executive Council objected to the increase. When the Assembly insisted on the restoration of the full tax, the Governor opted to dissolve the Legislature and call an election—three years before it was due. This seeming 'tempest-in-a-teapot' marked the beginning in Nova Scotia of the movement that ultimately led to responsible government or local self-government for the colonies of British North America.

It was in the midst of this drive for reformed government that Alexander Keith was persuaded by his Tory friends to stand for public office in the general election of 1840. He had already served for several years as a commissioner of the court of common pleas and as a justice of the peace. The election of 1840 was fought in the midst of the struggle for responsible government.[1]

At that time, Halifax County, like other large counties, was represented by more than one member (four in the case of Halifax County) in the House of Assembly. In a general election, each party would normally put up four candidates, of whom two would come from the town, and two from the rural area of the county.

In 1840, the Tories knew they were going to be hard-pressed to be successful. So they decided to run only two candidates, one in town and one in the country, in the hope that the voters would be attracted by the popularity of these individuals, personally, and would split their vote between Reform and Tory candidates and elect the two Tories.[2] Accordingly, they ran the well-known lawyer and writer, Beamish Murdoch, who had previously served as a member of the assembly, and the popular brewer, Alexander Keith.

Being a newcomer with little experience, Keith let Murdoch take the lead in putting forth the Tory case. Keith's main contributions were his ability to mix with people and his personal popularity. Unfortunately for Alexander Keith, the Reformers were just too strong in Halifax that year: they led the polls, and both Murdoch and Keith were defeated, with Keith, in fact, trailing the pack!

Fortunately, this first foray into politics did not turn Keith against public service. As a business and community leader, he felt a duty to make a contribution to public service. Until 1841, Halifax was not formally incorporated as a city, with its own municipal government. During the course of the 1830s, Joseph Howe emerged as the leader of the demand for popular reform in Nova Scotia. His prominence was greatly enhanced in 1835 when he publicly accused non-elected leaders of the government of corruption and incompetence. When these people had Howe charged with criminal libel, he opted for a trial by jury, represented himself in court and won a great victory. After that, Howe became a hero to the middle classes, and a continuing thorn in the side of the Governor and his circle of appointed advisors.

In addition to calling for reform of the provincial government, Howe argued that Halifax should be governed by a popularly elected municipal government. Most people, including the

Joseph Howe, 1854.

Courtesy of the Public Archives of Nova Scotia.

governor, agreed with him. The unanswered question in 1840 was who should be qualified to vote and to hold office.[3] Even Howe and his supporters believed that there should be minimum property qualifications for both voters and office holders.

In due course, the Governor agreed to grant a charter to the City of Halifax, but one that left power in the hands of the wealthier members of the community. To be eligible to vote, a man (women were not considered) had to own real property valued at no less than £20. To run for mayor or council, one had to have a net worth of £500-£1000. Even though it was Howe's intention that these restrictive eligibility requirements would gradually be reduced, it meant that for the first years, only a very small percentage of the population would get to vote, and an even smaller number would be eligible for office. There was no direct election of the Mayor. Rather, the Council elected the mayor from amongst its members. Clearly, control of the civic government was in the hands of the wealthy members of the community.

The first Mayor of Halifax, elected in May, 1841, was Stephen Binney, a 36-year old merchant with lots of money and from a Loyalist background. Binney loved the pomp and ceremony of his new office. He immediately insisted that he be referred to as the "Lord Mayor of Halifax"! Alexander Keith, elected to the first City Council in 1841 as a councilor for Ward Two, thus served on the first City Council. He was re-elected the following year. At that time, elections were held annually in September. The term ran from October through the following September. In 1842, he was elected as Alderman for Ward 2.

On October 3, 1843, Keith was chosen "unanimously" by his fellow councilors and aldermen to serve as Mayor. He was again elected Mayor in 1852. By that time, it was by popular vote, which Keith won 609 to 447.[4]

It was as Mayor, on May 23, 1844, that Keith had the privilege of accepting a brand new 417-pound fire bell for the Halifax Fire Station on Grand Parade, a gift from the Sun Fire Company. In presiding over the occasion, a task which he both enjoyed and performed admirably, Keith stated that he hoped "most sincerely, that there may be seldom occasion for the use of this liberal present, but (I) feel assured, should it be required, it will be found most efficient."[5]

During the 1840s, Queen Victoria (on the advice of her representative in Nova Scotia, Governor Falkland) appointed Alexander Keith to be a member of the Legislative Council. Many accounts indicate that this was in 1843. However, Keith is not mentioned in Minutes of the Executive Council until January 10, 1846, on which date, the minutes note, Alexander Keith took his seat in the chamber for the first time. It is possible that he was appointed in 1843, but did not take up his seat until 1846.[6]

The Legislative Council was the upper house of Nova Scotia's Legislature, its role modeled on that of the House of Lords in England. One contemporary described this role as follows:

Now they are legislators—tomorrow they are the arbiters of

Legislative Council Chamber.

Courtesy of the Public Archives of Nova Scotia.

> life and death—or the distributors of patronage. They form a Court of appeal in which the decisions of the gravest Judges of the land may be reviewed and reversed—and then they are suddenly changed to a Court of Marriage and Divorce.... On all occasions they surround the Representative of Her Majesty, who in most cases does, and in many is bound to, act by their advice, and one of the Members succeeds him when he is absent.[7]

As the upper house of the legislature, the Council could introduce legislation and had to approve bills passed by the House of Assembly in order for them to become law.

The Legislative Council was referred to as the "Council of Twelve", reflecting its membership. It was modeled after the House of Lords, except that there was no official aristocracy in

Alexander Keith as President of Legislative Council, 1868.

Courtesy of the Public Archives of Nova Scotia.

Nova Scotia.

About the time Alexander Keith was appointed to the Council, members of the Assembly were calling for the Legislative Council to be elected. But, neither King, Queen or Governor was ready for that. The Council saw itself as a necessary go-between, seeking to bring together, in consensus as it were, such divergent views as might exist between the Governor and Executive Council (i.e. the cabinet), on the one hand, and the House of Assembly, on the other.[8] Members of the Legislative Council, it should be noted, were not paid. This was to ensure:

> Gentlemen of sufficient means to keep up the independent character of the Body, and to render unnecessary the resort

Halifax, 1842.

Courtesy of the Public Archives of Nova Scotia.

to paid Members.[9]

Nevertheless, the membership of the Council, selected, as it was, by the Governor, tended to reflect his opinions, as well as the interests of the wealthy.

The Council was presided over by a President, who acted as a chair and speaker. Alexander Keith served as President of the Legislative Council from 1867 until his death in 1873.

Shortly after accepting this post, and following Confederation, Keith was offered a seat in the new Canadian Senate, but declined. The offer was initiated by Charles Tupper in recognition of Keith's support of Confederation.

In both the federal and provincial elections of 1867, Anti-Confederates, led by Howe and fellow newspaper publisher, William Annand, swept the polls, winning all but one seat in the House of Commons, and two in the House of Assembly. They also enjoyed a twenty per cent lead in the popular vote. From his position of leadership in the Legislative Council, Keith sought to block secessionist initiatives brought before the Council, and was able to do so for some time.[10]

Sir Charles Tupper, as premier of Nova Scotia, led the province into Confederation.

Courtesy of the Public Archives of Nova Scotia.

Alexander Keith: Confederate Agent and Southern Sympathizer?

Looking back in history, most people see the American Civil War of 1861-1865 as a conflict over whether there should be slavery in the United States. The Southern States that joined together and declared their independence believed that slavery was essential to their economy and way of life. People of the more industrialized northern states believed that slavery was an evil.

Officially, Nova Scotia, along with the rest of the British Empire, was neutral in what proved to be a long and bloody war. When the war broke out during the spring of 1861, it was not surprising that most Nova Scotians, given their close ties to New England, and impressed with President Abraham Lincoln's call for support and his articulation of principles of righteousness in his inaugural address, tended to support the Northern cause.

However, not long into the war, the Confederacy sent agents to British North America, including to Nova Scotia, to whip up support for the South. They sought to convince people that, having defeated the Confederacy, the Union (Northern) Army would be turned on the colonies of British North America, and would force them to do what they had opted not to do during the American Revolution, namely, join the United States. The result was that many people in Nova Scotia became increasingly sympathetic to the Southerners, who seemed far more civilized and sympathetic to the British Empire.[11]

A group of Halifax citizens soon emerged as leading supporters of the Southern cause. One of the most prominent was a man called Alexander Keith. This has led several historians and writers to assume that Alexander Keith, the brewer and subject of this book, was in fact a Southern sympathizer. And indeed, Alexander Keith, the Southern supporter and activist turned out to be quite the notorious villain and character. His activities, and those of his co-conspirators led to Halifax being described by more recent writers as "a center of treason" and "as seccession-minded as Richmond."[12]

This Alexander Keith, who called himself Alexander Keith, Jr., set up a business to profit from the War by accessing and selling supplies to the Confederacy. He also acquired a ship, *Cal-*

edonia, which he used to run the Northern blockades of Southern ports.[13] At one point, he was even arrested in Halifax as part of a mob, which sought to obstruct justice by helping a charged pirate escape.

Civil War activities were only some of the nefarious activities in which this Alexander Keith engaged. He is believed to have died in the German port of Bremerhaven, in December, 1875, from injuries suffered from an explosion on board the ship, *Mosel*, which was caused by a bomb in a trunk, which Keith had set himself, with the intent that it would explode after he had left the ship.

The issue of this villainous Alexander Keith's identity has been clarified in an article by writer/historian Pat Lotz of Halifax.[14] It turns out this Alexander Keith was, in fact, a nephew of Alexander Keith the brewer and leading citizen of Halifax. Alexander Keith, the villain, was the eldest son of John and Christiana Keith, and the nephew of our Alexander Keith. He did live with and work for his uncle early in life, but had left his uncle's employ and moved to the Halifax Hotel prior to the Civil War.

The research of historian, David Flemming, has established that at least six Alexander Keiths lived in Halifax between 1860 and 1990.[15]

So, the mystery is no longer a mystery, and the Honourable Alexander Keith was indeed an honourable man.

CSS *Tallahassee* in Halifax Harbour, 1864.

From the collection of the Maritime Museum of the Atlantic, Halifax, Nova Scotia, Canada.

Halifax Harbour at Sunset,
c.1853.

Collection of the Art Gallery of Nova Scotia.

CHAPTER 5

Man of the Home and Community

Shortly after Keith moved his business from Argyle Street to Lower Water Street, he embarked on another journey of some significance: on December 17, 1822, he married Sara Ann Stalcup of Halifax. Sadly, Sarah died within a decade at the age of 36 in 1832. Her obituary noted that she died of "a very painful illness, which she bore with patient resignation to the Divine will."[1] There were no children.

On September 30, 1833, Keith married his cousin, Eliza Keith, also of Halifax and youngest daughter of his father's brother, David Keith. Eliza and Alexander had nine children, two sons and seven daughters. Of these, only four lived to adulthood. Among those who did not survive was their first son, Alexander Keith, Jr., who was born August 9, 1836 and died May 16, 1837. Donald George Keith (1838-1886) succeeded his father at the brewery. Donald was not the entrepreneur that his father had been. Nor did he ever marry or have children.

On Donald's death at the young age of 43, he was succeeded at the brewery by his sister, Margaret Louise, who was married to Dr. William N. Wickwire of Kings County. They relocated to Halifax and he became Honourary Consul for the Netherlands, and eventually gave up medicine to assist in operating the brewery. Margaret Louise and her husband were married in 1870, and their marriage only ended with the death of Dr. Wickwire in 1922. They had two children, Blanche Adelia (1875-1911) who married Captain H. M. Elliott in 1899, and William Keith Wickwire (1876-1928), who married Annie Whitehead in 1912. Both marriages produced children, which, over two generations, have left descendents of Alexander Keith in Nova Scotia and elsewhere.

Alexander and Eliza Keith had two other daughters, Marjorie Eliza and Alexandrina, who lived their adult lives in England, the

Children of Alexander and Eliza Keith

Eliza Ann (1834-1835)
Alexander (1836-1837)
Donald George (1838-1886)
Eleanor Jane (1840-1873)
Margaret Louise (1844-1930)
Alexandrina Isabella (1846-1897)
Marjorie Elizabeth (1848-?)
Ann Emelia (1850-1854)
Emma Georgina (1853-1855)

latter married to a Lord Huddleston of Cambridge.[2]

As the husband of a successful and wealthy businessman, Eliza Keith would have found her career in managing house and home, in raising the children, and in supporting and accompanying her husband as social dictates of the times required. In carrying out her responsibilities, she would have been supported by a variety of servants. Women of wealth and station had opportunities, especially in widowhood or when their husbands were away, to manage family interests, in business as well as in the home. Margaret Louise, her daughter was an example of a woman who provided leadership in the family business. Some also were active in benevolent organizations, especially ones established by women, such as the Methodist Female Benevolent Society.

Women of less fortunate circumstances faced challenges of a different sort. They, of course had to attend to their homes and children, but without benefit of servants. Their meals and clothes were less elaborate, their tasks more mundane: washing and cleaning, sewing, knitting, weaving, chopping wood for the fire or taking in the coal, tending the garden (if they were so fortunate as to have one), baking, preserving and preparing the meals—often having to make do with considerably less than a home like Keith Hall. In the rural areas outside Halifax, women worked side by side with their husbands, fathers and brothers in the various tasks that had to be done on the farm, or in harvesting the sea. Milking the cows and tending to the chickens were a given. Some also had to take menial employment, serving others or taking in wash. Few professional careers were open to women, one of the few being the low-paid teaching profession.

The Old Pedlar, 1859.
Collection of the Art Gallery of Nova Scotia.

These women did not have their social calendars filled with fancy balls and dinners, but in maintaining hearth and home, and visiting with friends and relatives. Some were active in the church, for example, teaching Sunday school. A major part of the ordinary woman's world was in bearing and rearing children. During the 1820s, the average wife produced 6.6 children, only some of whom lived to adulthood.[3]

Between the extremes of rich and poor was a more palatable existence—though not with any increased vocational opportunities for women outside the home. A servant girl, perhaps from the country or a poorer home in the city, would be available to

The Orphan.

Collection of the Art Gallery of Nova Scotia.

do the more menial chores, such as the wash. This could be quite the ceremony, as recalled by a Mrs. Lenoir in her 98th year. "Monday was wash day and in those early times washing was a ceremony. Early in the morning soiled clothing was collected in a basket and the servant girl—there were no maids then, just plain servant girls—went to Governor's Pasture to wash. (It) was away up at the end of Barrington Street, near Africville. There was plenty of water there ... (and was) quite a sight. Little fires were kindled all around and white clothes adorned the green grass and bushes... Young people looked on the affair as a glorified picnic and enjoyed it. When 8 o'clock in the evening came, spotless clothes were re-packed in the baskets, the team arrived and the servant girls with their washes departed in state."[4]

Not all marital situations were happy, then as now. Unlike in the Colonies of Upper and Lower Canada, divorce was an option in Nova Scotia. Divorce laws were passed in 1758 and 1791, which provided, under certain circumstances, an opportunity for escape from unhappy marriages.[5] In 1857, Nova Scotia became the first colony in British North America to allow a divorce on the ground of cruelty.[6] While divorce provided escape from an unhappy situation for both men and women, the fall-out from such a decision was likely to be more challenging for women, who not likely having had the same access to education as their husbands, would find themselves with less enticing opportunities post-divorce. During Alexander Keith's day, women were not accepted into any college or university in the Maritimes. The first degree was not granted to a woman in the region until 1875. As a matter of fact, this female graduate was the first in the British Empire! Prior to that, women wishing advanced educations had to go to the United States.

In addition to his devotion to his family, Alexander Keith devoted considerable time, energy and commitment to charitable, fraternal and cultural organizations. Principal among them were the North British Society, the Highland Society of Nova Scotia, and the Masonic Order. Together with the various churches, in particular the evangelical churches, such organizations provided assistance to the poor and disadvantaged, particularly amongst desperate immigrants.

The religious organizations, in particular, were driven by their belief that those favoured with privilege and affluence had a 'Christian obligation', as it were, to share with those less fortunate. It was their belief that poverty was not a societal evil that could be overcome through political interventionist action so much as an inevitable condition inflicted on the less fortunate in society. Their activity was thus not so much targeted at political, social reform, as in directly providing relief from the effects of poverty.[7]

By the 1830s, the numbers of poor people arriving as immigrants in Halifax were causing sufficient concern as to create negative feelings about immigration generally. Little public support was provided, other than through prisons, like Bridewell, which were in deplorable condition, or the Halifax Poor Asylum, for those considered beyond mental redemption.

Some of the evangelical organizations also focused their attention to the plight of Afro-Americans and Aboriginal people.

Selling Mayflowers on the Market Place, 1872.

Collection of the Art Gallery of Nova Scotia.

Black refugees after the War of 1812 were not accorded the same benefits as their Caucasian counterparts. Many were denied land and forced into wage labour in the city.[8] Those whose ancestors had come as Loyalists had been settled in ghettoized communities, for the most part outside of Halifax, and were given what was considered inferior land. By mid-century, they comprised less than 2% of the population of Nova Scotia.

Aboriginals were in decreasing numbers, and not expected to survive as a people. The primary interest in them, on the part of the evangelicals, was the saving of their souls. While extinction did happen to the Beothuks in Newfoundland, the Mik'maq of Nova Scotia were of sufficient numbers that they did survive. Today, they are considerably more numerous than they were two centuries ago.

The North British Society was possibly the first ethno-cultural organization in Nova Scotia. It was founded on March 26,

Sketch taken from Dartmouth, c. 1834.

Collection of the Art Gallery of Nova Scotia.

1768 at Halifax—on the same day as the Saint Andrew's Lodge of Free and Accepted Masons.

The purpose of the Society was "the assistance of Scottish emigrants landing in the colony, and the establishment of a medium of communication with kindred Societies in the neighbouring provinces, as well as the maintenance of friendly feeling among Scotsmen resident in the community, and those who visited the country for the purposes of trade.

(The Society) gave to the emigrant the assistance which he could not otherwise have found in a strange country, and which in many cases led to success and fortune. It relieved the distressed, nurtured a patriotic feeling, and co-operated, to a moderate extent, with such institutions as the Thistle Society of New York, the Saint Andrew's

The Procession Passing beneath the Arch of the North British Society, 1878.
Collection of the Art Gallery of Nova Scotia.

Society of Philadelphia and the Scot Charitable Society of Boston."[9]

Alexander Keith was admitted to membership at the annual meeting of 1822. He was active and rose quickly through its ranks. In 1827, he was appointed to the executive as a member of the "Committee of Charity" on which he served until 1830. In that year, he was elected Vice-President, and the following year, became President for the year 1831. Terms of office were normally confined to a single year, and the organization encouraged the active participation and leadership of its younger members—nobody over the age of 45 was admitted to membership.[10]

The North British Society required its members to adhere to a strict code of conduct. For example, in addition to the age restriction, prospective members had to be of "good health, not of scandalous character, and not a Protestant—unless he be chosen by a majority of the members present and voting"[11] The Society met monthly, and sought to provide support to Scottish immigrants and visitors in any way they could. They particularly sought to provide support to members who became sick, and even covered the cost of a member's funeral (provided he had been a paid up member for at least a year).

The Annals of the Society list the names of 191 members at the 100th Anniversary meeting in 1868: 18 perpetual members, 120 ordinary members (of whom Alexander Keith was one), and 53 honorary members. Although Keith was a member for over fifty years, he was never made an 'honourary' member. His son Donald was admitted to membership in 1868, and served for a year on the 'Committee of Charity' in 1870, but did not follow his father to more senior offices within the Society.

The Highland Society of London was established in 1778. Sir Colin Campbell, later Lieutenant-Governor of Nova Scotia, was elected to membership in 1807. Subsequent chapters were established in other parts of Britain and the overseas colonies. The purpose of the Society was "the diffusion of useful knowledge, the relief of distressed Highlanders at a distance from their native homes, the improvement and general welfare of the Northern parts of the Kingdom, and the preservation of the martial, spirit, language, music and antiquities of Ancient Caledonians."[12]

The Highland Society placed a significant emphasis on " promoting patriotism and liberal views." The Society also reflected the Scots commitment to education in its priorities.

In 1838, Lieutenant -Governor Colin Campbell was given a commission by the appropriate authorities in London to establish a chapter of the Highland Society in Nova Scotia. In promoting the idea of the Society for Nova Scotia, he and his early supporters, who included such leading public figures as William Young (who subsequently served as Premier of Nova Scotia), Charles Wallace and James McNab, pointed out the benefits to Nova Scotia, and especially to Nova Scotians of Scottish origin: "very important benefits may be realized from a connection with so eminent and influential a body. Their views are of no narrow or sectarian cast. It is at once their pride and their ambition, as it ought to be, of every true son of Caledonia, to improve the moral condition, and by extending the blessings of education, to elevate the character of Scotsmen and their descendents. The distinction between Highlander and Lowlander is forgotten in a generous emulation to do good."[13]

It was natural that the new Highland Society of Nova Scotia would draw its initial membership from the membership roles of the North British Society. One of those was Alexander Keith. And it would seem that a close and complementary relationship developed between the two organizations. In view of the important contribution of the North British Society in providing support and 'charity' to needy persons, the leaders of the new Highland Society decided that their focus should and would be on improving education and educational opportunity for the Scots population of Nova Scotia, particularly the young. A great need was identified for both teachers and books, especially in the newer, rural communities and in Cape Breton. They estimated that some 50,000 young Nova Scotians of Scottish origin were in need of improved educational opportunity. And, as was noted by the *British Colonist*, "every family who are taught the elements of learning, become more useful and valuable to the community."

It was decided that the central organization of the Highland Society of Nova Scotia would be in Halifax, with branches organized in various parts of the Province. Each would be devoted to the cause of education among Scottish settlers, "whether Highland or Lowland, Catholic or Protestant".

Keith's activity in the Highland Society was over many years. In 1868, he was given the honour of election as Chief of the Society.

During the course of his career, Alexander Keith was also active in the Halifax Mechanics Library and the Auxiliary Colonial Society. But, the organization with which his name is most associated is the Masons, the Grand Lodge of Nova Scotia. In all, he was active in the Masonic fraternity in Britain, in the Maritimes and in Newfoundland for 57 years.

Freemasonry is one of the world's oldest secular fraternal

Masonic Temple, Liverpool, 1873.

Collection of the Art Gallery of Nova Scotia.

societies.[14] "It is a society of men concerned with moral and spiritual values. It members are taught its precepts by a series of ritual dramas, which follow ancient forms and use stonemasons' customs and tools as allegorical guides." Membership is open to any man of any race or religion, providing that he acknowledges or has a belief in a supreme or divine being. Freemasonry is not a religion itself, but a prerequisite to membership is a commitment that each member would practice his own religion. The aura of secrecy is often associated with the Masons, but, in fact, what is maintained as private or secret amongst Masons are traditional modes of recognition, as one to another.

MASONRY IS SIMPLE BROTHERLY LOVE, RELIEF AND TRUTH!

Masonry, the world's oldest and most respected Fraternity, encourages good men to become better men by promoting a life devoted to high ideals, community service and benevolence.

Hon. Alexander Keith.

Courtesy of the Public Archives of Nova Scotia.

Masons are expected to live their lives in accordance with three fundamental principles:

- brotherly love, tolerance and respect toward others,
- charity, caring and giving to others and giving through voluntary efforts, and
- commitment to the truth and high moral standards.

Freemasonry, from its origins, has been concerned with orphans, and with the sick and the aging.

Freemasonry is non-political: the discussion of politics is not allowed at Masonic meetings.

In sum, "a Freemason is encouraged to do his duty first to God (by whatever name he is known) through his faith and religious practice, and then, without detriment to his family and those dependent on him, to his neighbor through charity and service." Masons do not claim ownership of these values only that part of their commitment as members of the order is to honour and follow them.

Alexander Keith actually joined the Masons while still living in Sunderland, England, on July 23, 1816. He was 21 at the time and would remain a member of the Order until the day of his death in 1873. In Sunderland, he was an active participant in its fortnightly meetings at the Duke of Wellington, Low Street. Before leaving England, Keith was made a Senior Deacon of the Lodge, and was entitled to wear badges indicative of the same.

Immediately on arriving in Halifax, Keith affiliated with the Virgin Lodge #2 on the Provincial Registry. He remained a member of this particular Lodge for the rest of his life, during which time he held virtually every office in the organization. According to Masonic records, he was a very active and positive contributor to the activities of the organization.[15]

Over the years, Keith moved steadily through the ranks and offices of the Masonic Order, from Grand Deacon (Nova Scotia), 1825, to Grand Marshall (1827), to Junior Grand Warden (1828), to first Senior Grand Warden (1829-1837), to Deputy Grand Master (1837). In 1840, His Royal Highness, the Duke of Sussex, by letters patent elevated Keith to "head of the craft in Nova Scotia" (September, 1840) and later the same year (December, 1840), he was proclaimed Provincial Grand Master.

In 1847, Keith's territory was extended to include Prince

The Progress of the Prince of Wales in British North America, 1860.

Collection of the Art Gallery of Nova Scotia.

Edward Island, New Brunswick and Newfoundland. He continued to serve in this office until 1869.

On July 19, 1850, the Freemasons celebrated the 100th Anniversary of their founding by Lord Cornwallis in Nova Scotia. A great parade and review was held, presided over by their Grand Master, Alexander Keith. It turned out to be a beautiful day, and the various Lodges proceeded through the city to the Hollis Street residence of the Grand Master. Three cheers were called for the Grand Master and his wife, following which Keith laid the ceremonial corner stone for the expansion being built to the Masonic Hall.

During this period there were separate Grand Lodges for the English and Scottish Masonic Orders. However, throughout most of this period, Keith was Grand Master of both, even though technically they were rival organizations. Keith provided strong leadership to both, and needless to say, there was excellent harmony between the two supposed rivals throughout this period!

In 1865, Keith was honoured for his 25 years of leadership in the Masonic Order in the Atlantic colonies. He was presented with a great silver candelabrum, with three branches for lights, emblematic of Faith, Hope and Charity. In delivering the citation address, Deputy Grand Master James Forman said:

> The present state of Masonry in the Province exhibits a striking contrast to that which existed at the time you assumed your important functions: while the records of the Craft in 1840 exhibited but six Lodges holding warrants from the Grand Lodge of England, they now show twenty-two warranted lodges in efficient working order, and dispensations for the formation of two new lodges have been granted during the year.[16]

One of the more noteworthy of Keith's leadership accomplishments had been the establishment of a benevolent fund, for which had been raised the considerable sum of 400 pounds. These events concluded, similar remarks were made on behalf of the Scottish Order.

In responding to the presentation and speeches, Keith offered his heartfelt thanks, and, among other comments, said:

> If I have succeeded in performing the important duties of Provincial Grand Master satisfactorily to all, it is to be attributed, in no small degree, to the fact that I have ever received the cordial co-operation and assistance of my Grand Lodge officers and of the brethren generally, to all of whom I take this opportunity of expressing my obligations for the important services rendered me on all occasions....we may rest assured that amidst all the mutations of time and changes of circumstances it will stand 'a strong refuge' to the 'worthy Mason' in the hour of need or the storms of adversity, and will cheer the heart of the widow and the fatherless when misfortune leads them to feel the need of sympathy and the aid of friends.

In 1869, Alexander Keith was elected Grand Master of Masons for Nova Scotia, an office he held until his death. Throughout much of the later years of his life, Keith was by far the most prominent member of the Masonic Order in the Atlantic Colonies (thence Provinces). He made visits to various communities and Lodges about the region. Keith received many honours, among them: Honorary Member of the Grand Lodge of France, Royal Arch Mason in Royal Union Chapter #1, Grand Superintendent over Royal Arch Masonry in Nova Scotia, and in 1869, was unanimously elected and installed as Grand High Priest. He was made a Knight of the Temple in 1841, first Eminent Commander in 1858, and Provincial Grand Prior over the Atlantic Colonies in 1863.

Perhaps no event was more illustrative of the importance of the Masonic Order to Keith and of his leadership to the Order than when, in 1860, the Prince of Wales visited Halifax, and Keith opted to greet him with his Lodge brothers rather than in the higher station of the Legislative Council.

It was noted in a formal communication from the Grand Lodge, after Keith's death that:

> At the last annual meeting of Grand Lodge in June last (1873), he (Keith) expressed himself as still deeply interested in the welfare and prosperity of the Order, and willing to aid and assist the work by his counsel and advice, although, as he said, his age and infirmity prevented him from being with us in our assemblies as frequently as he wished. May the useful lessons that his long and active life set before us be lasting and beneficial to us. We may do well to be still more careful and considerate in our legislation and action in Masonic matters, knowing that the influence of his more mature ideas and judgment is no more at hand to give us direction.
>
> To his truly Masonic example and to the care with which he always inculcated sound Masonic precepts, it is in a large measure owing that Masonry has now taken so deep a hold upon society in this Province; that Masonic charity is being so largely and beneficially dispensed; and that even among those who are not of our Order our ancient and honorable institution commands universal respect. [17]

Alexander Keith standing in Masonic Arch, Halifax, 1860.

Courtesy of the Public Archives of Nova Scotia.

Col. Sidney Oland

Courtesy of the Oland Brewery

CHAPTER SIX

Alexander Keith's Legacy

Today, Keith Hall and Keith's Brewery are visual legacies of a Scottish immigrant of humble origin who came to Nova Scotia to seek his fortune, and did so with great success, while returning in full measure a major contribution to his adopted community and country. But buildings are only a part of the legacy of Alexander Keith.

Of course, Keith left a tangible legacy to the benefit of his family in an estate in excess of some $300,000—the equivalent of millions today. The entirety of his estate, including an annual income of 500 pounds, he left to his wife, with the exception of the brewery, which was to be sold and the proceeds divided into six shares, with two shares going to his son Donald, and one share each to his four surviving daughters. The will also stipulated that on the death of Mrs. Keith, Keith Hall and its contents were to be sold.

In fact, Alexander Keith and Son Ltd. remained in the family, run first by Donald, thence by his sister Margaret Louise. In July 1928, it was purchased by Col. Sidney Oland, giving that family a monopoly of the brewing industry in Nova Scotia.[1] However, recognizing the popularity of the Keith brand, they continued to run Alexander Keith and Son Ltd. as a separate brewery within the Oland family of companies. Similarly, when Olands was purchased by John Labatt Ltd. in June, 1971, the decision was taken by Labatt to retain the Oland's name and brand, and they named their new Nova Scotia company, Olands Breweries (1971) Ltd. Again, the Keith name also remained.[2]

These brand maintenance decisions, proved to be wise ones, as both the Oland and Keith brands were and continue to be very popular in the Maritime market. Today, Alexander Keith's India Pale Ale is Nova Scotia's biggest selling beer. Through its draft product, Keith's has been experiencing amazing growth right across Canada and in the United States.

After Olands was purchased by Labatts, the Keith's brewery ceased to be used as a brewery per se in 1972. However, during the summer of 2000, Alexander Keith's Nova Scotia Brewery was restored, at a cost of some $4 million. It has since been re-opened as a working brewery together with other historically restored premises, including a 19th century general store, and a brew house and tavern called "The Stag's Head." It has rapidly become a major tourist attraction in the historic part of the city, providing a fascinating tour of the original brewing process.

The leadership and the extent to which Keith played a major role in building charitable organizations, such as the Masonic Order and the North British Society, and the positive impact that they have had on the social and cultural development of Nova Scotia and the Maritimes, are also a part of the legacy of Alexander Keith.

It is hard to get the measure of a man whom one has never met and can never meet, and without the benefit of sound or television, as we have them today. Only from snippets in the press, and records from organizations such as the Masonic Order, can we gauge any real indication of what Keith was like as a person, and of what people thought of him at the time. Unfortunately, few personal papers and documents are available through traditional public repositories for such things.

Still, it is reasonable and possible to determine and conclude that Alexander Keith was an extraordinary person. His determination and business acumen is obvious from the success of his brewing enterprise and the number of other companies that sought the benefit of his wisdom through their Boards. His commitment to his community is obvious through his lengthy career of public service. And his adherence to principles of charity, justice and consideration for one's neighbours is evident from his commitment to and extensive career in the Masons, the North British Society and the Highland Society. Keith's words at his last Masonic annual meeting, quoted earlier, give personal testimony to his commitment to the ideals for which these fraternal organizations were established and exist.

Keith's funeral on December 17, 1873, was one of the largest ever held in Halifax to that day. It included a procession of virtu-

Mrs. Alexander Keith.
Courtesy of the Public Archives of Nova Scotia.

ally every community, provincial and Masonic leader from Nova Scotia. The funeral was attended by every dignitary of note in the city, as well as by hundreds, who, through Keith's enterprise, found careers and a good and steady living. Flags flew at half-staff, on every public, on most private buildings, as well as from all the ships in the harbour that day. The attending reporter for the *Acadian Recorder* wrote:

> It is a long time since any similar event has occurred in our city, which has to such an extent been a matter in which the whole people took a melancholy interest. The illustrious connection of the deceased with the Masonic

Alexander Keith's monument in Camp Hill Cemetary.

Photo by Gary Castle.

> Body had, of course, given him unusual claim to tokens of the highest respect, from a very large class in this or any other community; but besides this, Mr. Keith's name had become almost a household word in Halifax and beyond.
>
> It was not surprising, therefore, to find that a large concourse of people assembled in the neighbourhood of Mr. Keith's late residence on Hollis Street, to witness the funeral procession, which it was evident would be of an imposing nature.
>
> Since the death on Sunday, the body has been viewed by hundreds of persons, from the highest in the land, all anxious to take a last glimpse at one who was so well known and deservedly popular.[3]

The procession with full Masonic ritual, marshaled at 1pm, proceeded at 2pm from the residence on Hollis Street, north to George Street, up George to Barrington, south to Spring Garden Road, up Spring Garden Road to South Park, up South Park to Sackville Street and up Sackville to Camp Hill Cemetery, where Keith's great monument (the largest in that formidable and historic cemetery) remains today.

On the day of a funeral, the euphoria of the occasion often leads to the use of exaggerated commendation of the deceased. The benefit of time, often tempers recollections to some extent. Thus, it is of interest to note that, writing a retrospective on Alexander Keith in 1915, the Rev. Allan Pollok, who had known Keith well, described him as "the most hospitable man who ever lived in this city, … a man of the most generous disposition." In sum, there is no evidence to suggest that Alexander Keith was not, in every respect, an outstanding individual and, in every respect, a great Nova Scotian of the 19th century.

Today, they say of Alexander Keith's beer, "those who like it, like it a lot." Well, it would seem that to have known the Honourable Alexander Keith, was to like HIM a lot.

Panoramic View of the City of Halifax, 1899.

Collection of the Art Gallery of Nova Scotia.

Beer Making Today

According to the Brewers Association of Canada, the brewing process is partly art, partly science:
Brewing is fundamentally a natural process.
The art and science of brewing is in converting natural food materials into a pure, pleasing beverage.
Although the main ingredients of beer have remained constant, it is the precise recipe and timing of the brew that gives one a different taste from another.
Those ingredients include water, yeast, malt and hops.

For a detailed description of how beer is made, see either the web site of the Brewers Association of Canada (from which this quote is taken) www.brewers.ca/about_beer/process.htm, or
for a more detailed description, see www.keiths.ca

Notes and References

Introduction

1) Rev. Alan Pollock, quoted in the Halifax *Morning Chronicle*, c1936.

Chapter 1

1) See the web page: "What to See and Do in the Halkirk area," www.scotland-index.co.uk/caithness/in_halkirk.htm
2) From Reginald V. Harris, "Ruler of the Craft in Nova Scotia, 1839-1873," pamphlet published by the Grand Lodge of Nova Scotia, 1957.

Chapter 2

1) from "Beer Making in ancient Egypt," *Isis Unveiled*, p543, author unidentified, web site: www.blavatsky.net/russion/pebeer.htm)
2) from *Natural History*, 5/96, p 24, cited in *ibid.*
3) from *In Ancient Egypt, the Beer of Kings Was a Sophistocated Brew* by John N. Wilford, New York Times International A9, 7/26/96. cited in *ibid.*
4) This section is based on a two-part article called 'India Pale Ale, (Parts I & II): IPA and Empire', by Thom Tomlinson, in 'Brewing Techniques: brewing in Styles, www.brewingtechniques.com/library/styles/2_2style.html
5) 'Hops' is a plant, the fruit of which is used to give a bitter taste to the malt used in making beer.
6) Tomlinson, *op.cit.*, p5.
7) See Frank Emmerson, *The Scots*, Tantallon, Four East Publications, 1987, 14-23.
8) J. S. Martell, "Military Settlements in Nova Scotia after the War of 1812," *Collections*, N.S.H.S. Vol. 24, 1938, 78-80.
9) J. S. Martell, *Immigration to and Emigration from Nova Scotia, 1815-1838,* Halifax, Public Archives of Nova Scotia, 1942, p7. The specific information on immigration to Nova Scotia, with the exception of the note below is drawn from Martell's work.
10) Lesley Choyce, *Nova Scotia: Shaped by the Sea*, Toronto, Viking Press, 1996, pp152-153.
11) Peter Lynch, "Early Reminiscences of Halifax: Men Who Have Passed From Us," *Collections*, N.S.H.S., Vol. 16, 1912, 175-176.

Chapter 3

1) See article by Claudia Pinsent, *The Chronicle-Herald*, PANS, MG100, Vol. 61, #29.
2) This issue is presented and given an overview in J. Fingard, J. Guilford

and D. Sutherland, *Halifax: The First 250 Years*, Halifax, Formac Publishing Company, 1999, Chapter 3, pp 43-66.
3) Ibid., 43-44.
4) Reginald Harris, *op.cit.* p 2.
5) Ibid., 45.
6) Peter Lynch, *op.cit.*, 173-175.
7) Peter Lynch, "Early Reminiscences of Halifax," *Collections*, N.S.H.S., Vol.17, 1913, 120-126.
8) Novascotian, April 30, 1834.
9) Philip Girard, "The Rise and Fall of Urban Justice in Halifax, 1815-1886," *Nova Scotia Historical Review,* Vol. 8 #2, 1988, 57-71.
10) The material for this feature was drawn from: Horace A. Flemming, "Halifax Currency," *Collections*, N.S.H.S., Vol. 20, 1921, 111-138.
11) Novascotian, June 29, 1836, p206.
12) Novascotian, June 29, 1836, p 206.
13) Pinsent, *op.cit.*
14) Reginald V. Harris, *op.cit.*, p 2
15) David Flemming in correspondence to the author, February 23, 2001.
16) Novascotian, November 6, 1854.
17) The Colonist, September 3, 1863. See also unpublished article by Edith M. Creighton, "Four Stories in Stone: Keith Hall. Available at www.alexander-keiths.com/theman .
18) Susan Buggey, "Building Halifax," *Acadiensis,* Vol. , 19 , pp 99-100.
19) Edith Creighton, *op.cit.*, p3 (un-numbered).

Chapter 4

1) The concept of responsible government is the principle that those charged with governing (the advisors to the Governor [the Queen/King's representative], the Executive Council) should be chosen from amongst the majority party in the elected legislature. It is the principle of responsible government that makes Canada and Nova Scotia truly democratic.
2) See J. Murray Beck, *Politics of Nova Scotia, 1710-1896*, Tantallon, Four East Publications, 1985, chapter 5, pp 101-130, and Brian Cuthbertson, *Johnny Bluenose at the Polls*, Halifax, Formac Publishing, 1994, pp 72-74.
3) See David Sutherland, "A Prince, the Governor and Mr. Mayor," *Journal of the Royal Nova Scotia Historical Society*, Vol I, 1998, pp 93-103.
4) David Flemming to Peter McCreath, Feb. 25, 2001, from information gathered from newspapers.
5) The Halifax Times, May 28, 1844.

6) David Flemming, *ibid.*
7) Alexander Stewart, quoted in *Novascotian*, February 27, 1834. Cited in J. Murray Beck, *The Government of Nova Scotia*, Toronto, University of Toronto Press, 1957, p100.
8) Beck, *ibid.*, p102.
9) Ibid.
10) K. G. Pryke, entry on Alexander Keith, *Dictionary of Canadian Biography*, Vol. 10, 1871-1880, Toronto, University of Toronto Press, 1972, p395.
11) See Harry A. Overholtzer, "Nova Scotia and the United States Civil War, 1861-1865," MA Thesis, Dalhousie University, 1965, pp 8-10, 18-20, 24.
12) Cited in Francis I. W. Jones, "A Hot Southern Town: Confederate Sympathizers in Halifax during the American Civil War," *Journal of the Royal Nova Scotia Historical Society*, Vol 2, 1999, pp 52-69.
13) Pat Lotz, "Alexander Keith a Criminal? Exploding the Myth," *Griffin*, Heritage Trust of Nova Scotia, March, 1997, pp 10-11, 15.
14) Ibid.
15) Correspondence with the author, February 23, 2001.

Chapter 5

1) Acadian Recorder, August 24, 1832.
2) R.V. Harris, *op.cit.*, p17.
3) Ia. Ross Robertson, "The 1850s: Maturity and Reform," in *The Atlantic Region to Confederations: A History*, Edited by Phillip A. Buckner and John G. Reid, Toronto and Fredericton, University of Toronto Press and Acadiensis Press, 1994, p351.
4) T. W. Acheson, "The 1840s: Decade of Tribulations," in Buckner and Reid, *op.cit.*, p321.
5) Cited in Judith Fingard, "The 1820s: Peach, Privilege, and the Promise of Progress," in Buckner and Reid, *op.cit.*, p281.
20) P. H. Lenoir (as told to Mrs. William Dennis), *Collections*, N.S.H.S., Vol. 23, 1936, p5.
6) Judith Fingard, *op.cit.* ("The 1820s), pp272-274.
7) Ibid., p275.
8) James L. Macdonald, *Annals of the North British Society, 1768-1903*, Halifax, 1905, p2.
9) Ibid., pp 156, 171, 183, 187.
10) Ibid., p3.
11) Nova Scotia Royal Gazette, May 30, 1838, p3.
12) Ibid.
13) The description here of the Freemasons, what they are and for

what they stand are taken from the web site of the United Grand Lodge of England http://thelonious.mit.edu/Masonry/Essays/ugl-whatis.html

14) A detailed recitation of Keith's activities in the Masonic Order in Nova Scotia is provided in Reginal Harris, *Alexander Keith: Ruler of the Craft in Nova Scotia*, 1839-1873, from which the information provided here is derived.

15) Ibid., p7.

16) Ibid., p14.-15.

Chapter 6:

1) G. Brenton Haliburton, *What's Brewing*, Tantallon, Four East Publications, 1994, p 45.

2) Ibid., p79.

3) Acadian Recorder, December 17, 1873, p2, col.6.

Selected Bibliography

Books

J. Murray Beck, *The Government of Nova Scotia*, Toronto, University of Toronto Press, 1957, xii, 372.

J. Murray Beck, *Joseph Howe: Volume I: Conservative Reformer, 1804-1848*, Kingston and Montreal, Queens-McGill University Press, 1982, viii, 389.

J. Murray Beck, *Politics of Nova Scotia, 1710-1896*, Tantallon, Four East Publications, 1985, 300.

Phillip A. Buckner and John G. Reid, Editors, *The Atlantic Region to Confederation: A History*, Edited by Toronto and Fredericton, University of Toronto Press and Acadiensis Press, 1994, 491.

Lesley Choyce, *Nova Scotia: Shaped by the Sea*, Toronto, Viking Press, 1996, 305.

Brian Cuthbertson, *Johnny Bluenose at the Polls*, Halifax, Formac Publishing, 1994, vii, 344.

Frank Emmerson, *The Scots*, Tantallon, Four East Publications, 1987, 70.

Judith Fingard, Janet Guildford, David Sutherland, *Halifax: the First 250 Years*, Halifax, Formac Publishing, 1999, 192.

G. Brenton Haliburton, *What's Brewing: Oland, 1867-11971: A History*, Tantallon, Four East Publications, 1994, ix, 96.

Thomas H. Raddall, *Halifax: Warden of the North*, Toronto, McClelland and Stewart Ltd., 1971, xvi, 343.

E. M. Saunders, *Three Premiers of Nova Scotia*, Toronto, William Briggs, 1909, 628.

Unpublished Theses

Harry A. Overholtzer, "Nova Scotia and the United States Civil War," MA Thesis, Dalhousie University, 1965.

Articles

T. B. Akins, "History of Halifax City," *Collections*, Nova Scotia Historical Society, Vol. VIII, 1895, 1-272.

P. Buchan, "The Catti: Ancient Tribe of the Keiths," from *The Ancient and Noble family of Keith*, 1820. Posted on http://people.ne.mediaone.net/thekeithclan/chattie.htm.

Susan Buggey, "Building Halifax, 1841-1871," *Acadiensis*, Vol. X, #1, Autumn, 1980, 90-122.

Edith M. Creighton, "Four Stories in Stone: Keith Hall," posted on www.alexander-keiths.com/theman/html .

David Flemming, "The Life and Times of Alexander Keith," unpublished, 2000, 2.

Horace A. Flemming, "Halifax Currency," *Collections*, N.S.H.S., Vol. 20, 1921, 111-138.

Reginald V. Harris, "Hon. Alexander Keith: Ruler of the Craft in Nova Scotia, 1839-1873," pamphlet published by the Grand Lodge of Nova Scotia, 1957, 17.

Francis I. W. Jones, "A Hot Southern Town: Confederate Sympathizers in Halifax during the American Civil War," *Journal*, Nova Scotia Historical Society, Vol. 2, 1999, 52-69.

P. H. Lenoir (as told to Mrs. William Dennis), *Collections*, N.S.H.S., Vol. 23, 1936, 1-14.

Pat Lotz, "Alexander Keith a Criminal? Exploding the myth," *The Griffin*, Heritage Trust of Nova Scotia, March, 1997, 10-11 & 15.

Peter Lynch, "Early Reminiscences of Halifax," *Collections*, N.S.H.S., Vol. 17, 1913, 120-126.

Peter Lynch, "Early Reminiscences of Halifax: Men Who Have Passed From Us," *Collections*, N.S.H.S., Vol. 16, 1912, 171-204.

J. S. Martell, *Immigration to and Emigration from Nova Scotia, 1815-1838*, Halifax, Public Archives of Nova Scotia, 1942, 112.

J. S. Martell, "Military Settlements in Nova Scotia after the War of 1812," *Collections*, N.S.H.S., Vol. 24, 1938, 75-106.

Claudia Pinsent, "He was a Busy Boy," Halifax *Chronicle-Herald*, available at PANS, MG100, Vol. 61, #29.

Roger Protz, "India Pale Ale," *Malt Advocate*, posted on http://realbeer.com/maltadvocate.html.

K. G. Pryke, "Alexander Keith," *Dictionary of Canadian Biography*, Vol. 10, 1871-1880, Marc La Terreur (editor), University of Toronto Press,

1972, 395-396.

David Sutherland, "A Prince, the Governor and Mr. Mayor," *Journal*, N. S.H. S., Vol. 1, 1998, 93-103.

Thom Tomlinson, "India Pale Ale, Parts I: IPA and Empire" and "India Pale Ale, Part II: The Sun Never Sets —", from *Brewing in Styles*, posted on com/library/styles.html" http://brewingtechniques.com/library/styles.html.

Restored Alexander Keith's Nova Scotia Brewery, 2000.

Courtesy of the Oland Brewery.

Collection Art Gallery of Nova Scotia

Pg. 3: 1995.191 Charles W. Torbett, *View of Halifax from Dartmouth Cove*, 1829, gift of John and Norma Oyler, Halifax.

Pg. 14: 1986.51 John E. Woolford, *A View of Halifax from Fort George*, 1817, purchased with funds from the Government of Canada under the terms of the Cultural Property Export and Import Act; the AGNS Gallery Shop; and Mr. and Mrs. Leroy J. Zwicker, Halifax, 1986.

Pg. 20: 1995.419.1 Artist unknown, *Wreck of the Emigrant Ship JOHN*, 1855 gift of John and Norma Oyler, Halifax.

Pg. 21: 1995.425 Charles Williams, *The English and Newfoundland Mail Vessels Making their Way through the Ice in Halifax Harbour*, 1859, gift of John and Norma Oyler, Halifax.

Pg. 22: 1998.410 William Eagar, *Tandem Club Assembling in front of Dalhousie College, NS*, 1842, gift of John and Norma Oyler, Halifax.

Pg. 26: 1995.257 W.O. Carlile, *The Soldier's Smoking Room*, 1872, gift of John and Norma Oyler, Halifax.

Pg. 28: 1995.429 H.H. Laird, *The Fire in Granville Street*, 1859, gift of John and Norma Oyler, Halifax.

Pg. 36: 1995.269 Joseph Rogers, *Residence of Hon. Alexander Keith*, 1872, gift of John and Norma Oyler, Halifax.

Pg. 42: 1994.258 John Poad Drake, *Shipping at Low Tide, Halifax*, c. 1820, purchase dedicated to the memory of Evan Petley–Jones.

Pg. 54: TL1989.2 John O'Brien, *Halifax Harbour at Sunset*, c. 1853, Halifax Board of Trade.

Pg. 57: 1930.2 William Raphael, *The Old Peddlar*, 1859.

Pg. 58: 1989.113 Thomas Faed, *The Orphan*, n.d., gift of Hugh and Suzanne Conrod, Dartmouth, in memory of Julian Jakobos.

Pg. 60: 1995.262 W.O. Carlile, *Selling Mayflowers on the Marketplace*, 1872, gift of John and Norma Oyler, Halifax.

Pg. 61: 1980.62 Robert Petley, *Sketch taken from Dartmouth*, c. 1834.

Pg. 62: 1995.506 H.A. Ogden, *The Procession Passing beneath the Arch of the North British Society*, 1878, gift of John and Norma Oyler, Halifax.

Pg. 65: 1995.109 D. Buchanan, *Masonic Temple, Liverpool*, 1873, gift of John and Norma Oyler, Halifax.

Pg. 68: 1995.436 G.H. Andrews, *The Progress of the Prince of Wales in British North America*, 1860, gift of John and Norma Oyler, Halifax.

Pg. 78: 1995.148 Albert Ruger, *Panoramic View of the City of Halifax*, 1879, gift of John and Norma Oyler, Halifax.

Family of Donald Keith & Christina Brims

Donald Keith (1767-1847)
(m Christina Brims)

David Keith (1774-1836) (brother of Donald)

Eliza Keith (1814-1895)
(m. Alexander Keith)
(1833)

David Keith

Alexander Keith
(1795-1873)
(m. Sarah Ann Scalcup)
(1822 - no children)
(m. Eliza Keith 1814-1895)

John Keith
(1799-1863}
(m. Christina)
(1812-1880)
6 Children

Donald Keith

Eliza Ann (1834-1835) (died as infant)
Alexander (1836-1837) (died as infant)
Donald George (1838-1886) (never married, no children)
Eleanor Jane ((1840-1873) (never married, no children)
Margaret Louise (1844-1930) — m. Dr. William N. Wickwire (1870) (1839-1922)
Alexandrina Isabella ((1846-1897) (m. Lord Huddleston, lived in London)
Marjorie Elizabeth (1848- ?) (never married, no children)
Ann Emelia (1850-1854) (died as child)
Emma Georgina (1853-1855) (died as infant)

Blanche Adelia Wickwire
(1875-1911)
m. (1899) Capt. H. M. Elliot

William Keith Wickwire
(1876-1928)
m. (1912) Annie Whitehead

Wickwire (1913) (died as infant)
William Alexander Keith Wickwire (1914-1946) (m. Jean Carey, no children)
Robert Donald Thomas Wickwire (1920-1987) (m. Audrey Eleanor Day)
Margaret Emma Wickwire (b1923) (m. Victor George King)
Blanch Louise

Greg King **(b. 1950)**
Randall King **(b.1954)**

Paul Wickwire **(b.1949)**
Ross Alex. Wickwire **(b. 1954)**

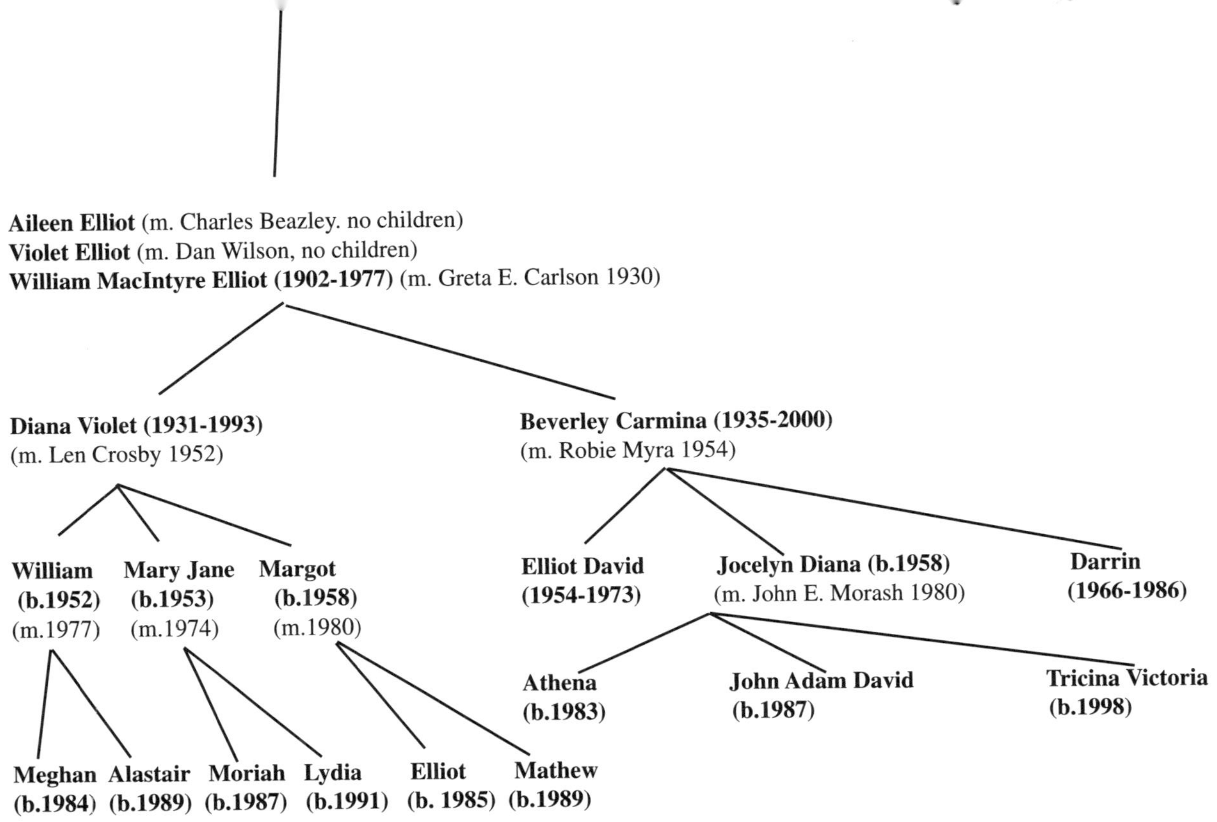

Aileen Elliot (m. Charles Beazley. no children)
Violet Elliot (m. Dan Wilson, no children)
William MacIntyre Elliot (1902-1977) (m. Greta E. Carlson 1930)
Diana Violet (1931-1993) (m. Len Crosby 1952)
Beverley Carmina (1935-2000) (m. Robie Myra 1954)
William (b.1952) (m.1977)
Mary Jane (b.1953) (m.1974)
Margot (b.1958) (m.1980)
Elliot David (1954-1973)
Jocelyn Diana (b.1958) (m. John E. Morash 1980)
Darrin (1966-1986)
Athena (b.1983)
John Adam David (b.1987)
Tricina Victoria (b.1998)
Meghan (b.1984)
Alastair (b.1989)
Moriah (b.1987)
Lydia (b.1991)
Elliot (b. 1985)
Mathew (b.1989)

Original tunnel connecting Keith's home to the brewery.

Courtesy of the Oland Brewery.